BEING
REAL

BEING
REAL

SHARING YOUR FAITH
WITHOUT LOSING YOUR FRIENDS

MIKE KIPP & KENNY WADE

[UNDERCURRENT SERIES]

Barefoot Ministries,
Kansas City, Missouri

BEING REAL

SHARING YOUR FAITH
WITHOUT LOSING YOUR FRIENDS

MIKE KIPP & KENNY WADE

{ UNDERCURRENT SERIES }

Barefoot Ministries®

Kansas City, Missouri

Copyright 2007
by Barefoot Ministries®

ISBN 978-0-8341-5020-1

Printed in the United States of America

Editors: Mike Wonch and Bo Cassell
Assistant Editor: Stephanie Harris
Cover Design: Lindsey Rohner
Interior Design: Sharon Page

Library of Congress Cataloging-in-Publication Data

Kipp, Mike, 1970-
     Being real : sharing your faith without losing your friends / by Mike Kipp and Kenny Wade.
          p. cm. — (Undercurrent series)
     Includes bibliographical references.
     ISBN 978-0-8341-5020-1
     1. Friendship—Religious aspects—Christianity. 2. Witness bearing (Christianity) I. Wade, Kenny, 1977-
II. Title.

     BV4647.F7K57 2007
     248'.5—dc22

                                                                                2007020968

10 9 8 7 6 5 4 3 2 1

Mike would like to dedicate this book to:

My wife Sandy, who has always been the pastor to this pastor—you are my gift from God and I daily thank Him for you, and to Spencer and McKenna, our children, who have taught me more about God's love in their short lives than I have learned through much study and effort.

Kenny would like to dedicate this book to:

- My wife and kids who remind me of God's kingdom every day;
- Every person I have tried to, am, or will share Jesus' grace with, in both good and tacky ways (with really good intentions). My heart is that we would all enter into God's kingdom and enjoy together great green pastures of grace, in this life, and the next; and
- Jesus. I thought I knew what You wanted me to give up for Lent this year: any unnecessary spending. I never dreamed You would be inviting me to add something to life instead: co-authoring this book.

ACKNOWLEDGEMENTS:

The authors would like to acknowledge and thank the following people:

Mike:

I would like to acknowledge my colleagues in the School of Theology and Christian Ministry at Northwest Nazarene University; you each have shaped, challenged, taught, and cared for me in ways you likely will never know.

And to the students in my classes during the spring semester 2007, who were aware of the scarcity of my time and yet were so patient and understanding. You will always be much more than my students, for you are my friends.

And finally to you the reader—may God's Spirit illuminate you to experience His freedom so you may truly live and be real.

Kenny:

I would like to thank my wife and kids for their direct contribution in this project by investing in me with love, grace, and patience. Debra—you teach me every day about Jesus' grace. Emily, Parker, and Braydon—you teach me about God's love by just being who God has created you to be.

The Pastoral Staff Team at Boise 1st Church of the Nazarene for many great Kingdom conversations, weekly.

The face2face youth ministry students and youth staff for putting up with a me as I was trying to balance life in the midst of this "good" storm.

The students in our youth ministry and on the Northwest district for contributing their evangelism experiences.

My neighbor Jennifer, for loving me and my family into the Kingdom.

Coffee and conversation with people Jesus uses to shape me: Mike Kipp (mentor and friend), Bob Diehm, Matt Boyd, Stuart Williams, and Big Picture Trainers, my Ma-and-Pa in Grace (inlaws). Vern and Kathy Emerson for listening; my parents, Ken and Carolyn Wade for prayers and advice; my extended family (especially my Grammie) for prayers of support, even when they don't know what they are praying for. My accountability partner, Joel Alsworth; my spiritual director, Trisha Nelson; Mark Yaconelli for great E-mail counsel.

Last, but first, I would like to thank Jesus, my Rabbi, Master, Lord and Friend for being crazy enough to invite me to be a part of something so beyond my qualifications.

May Jesus' Kingdom come. . . .

CONTENTS

CHAPTER 1

A LOOK AT EVANGELISM

SHOT OFF YOUR HORSE

Like a scene ripped from the dust and trail of the Old West, he'd been shot off his horse . . .

In January 2007, in a small eastern Oregon town, there was a real-life skirmish akin to an old West gun battle.[1] Some cattle with the wrong brand wound up in a rancher's herd. The rightful owner and his son saddled up and went to the spread "next door" to have a friendly conversation about straightening out the mistake.

Perched on their horses, they were approached by the un-rightful owner with his rifle in hand. He was accompanied by a female friend outside the house. Disdainful toward any implication that he might be rustling cattle or that said cattle may in fact not be his, the standing man proceeded to shoot the inno-cent owner from his mount. A tussle ensued between the second horseman and the shooter. During the dust-flinging altercation, the female witness yelled obscenities and called for the shooter to cave the defender's head in with a rock. I don't care who you are, that's a bad day on the ranch.

The heart of this book is not to shoot evangelism off its horse. This mission is one of reclaiming evangelism more as a way to *be*, than a way to *do*. In the journey of our conversation, we have gathered some insights from students in middle school, high school, university, a few volunteer youth workers, as well as full-time youth workers. Most have some form of church experience. Names and ages are listed where given. All were asked for permission to reuse this information.

GOOD, BAD AND UGLY

In the movie "The Good, the Bad and the Ugly," Clint Eastwood, a bounty hunter, and an outlaw find themselves faced off for a gunfight in the middle of a sun-baked graveyard, in search of buried wealth. That's what we are striving for here. In search of buried wealth under layers of evangelistic practices—seeking to reclaim what faith sharing is all about. Here are some perspectives on the evangelism experience we hope will stir up conversation and lead us to examine our methods and explore new approaches.

Each person was asked:

1) **What is the first thing that comes to mind when you hear the word *evangelism*?**

2) **In your view, what's the "good, bad, and ugly" of evangelism?**

Here is a collection of their responses:

Adult Leader (age 28)

Evangelism: sharing Christ's love.

Good: showing His love and it being received well.

Bad & Ugly: being yelled at and being called narrow-minded.

Teenager (age 17)

Evangelism: preaching Christ to everyone.

John (age 17) 🖋

Evangelism: missionaries.

Good: bring people to the Lord.

Bad: can break friendships.

Ugly: people can get hurt.

Sarah (age 17)

Evangelism: sharing the gospel, reaching out.

Good: sharing my stories of the miracles God has done in me and what I have seen; how amazing and awesome He is.

Evangelism Story: I was studying in a coffee shop and this guy who I had seen a few times started witnessing to me. I just let him go, because I kinda wanted to see what technique he used and what he had to say. NOT A GOOD IDEA (at least in this case). Well . . . it did show a lot of things—he made me mad. He pretty much rudely pointed out stuff I was doing wrong, some of which didn't make sense (some was true and I was working on it). He totally jumped to conclusions, and it really made me mad. This made me realize how we jump to conclusions and can offend people and turn away those who are not Christians. If I was not a Christian, I would have gone away, not wanting to have anything to do with a church. We can't just force ourselves on people. We are not above or better than anyone.

DeAnna (age 18)

Evangelism: outreach/reaching out.

Good: when you talk to someone about what they believe and then accept them and tell them about God if they ask, but they see Him through your acceptance of them.

Ugly: when people from other religions come to the door.

Youth Pastor (age 27)

Evangelism: responsibility.

Good: somebody hearing the message.

Bad: somebody not choosing the message.

Ugly: nobody sharing the message.

Karissa (age 13)

Evangelism: people helping.

Good: help my friends at church.

Ugly: when people from other religions come to the door.

Lauren (age 14)

Evangelism: my aunt and uncle in Ecuador.

Good: went there to help build a house.

Scott (age 34) Youth Worker

Evangelism: go!

Good: brings people to Christ.

Bad: scares some people away.

Ugly: no follow-up after the people are brought to Christ.

David (age 14)

Evangelism: stained-glass window, a lot of little pieces fittin' together to make a big picture.

James (age 28) Youth Pastor

Evangelism: I think I was raised to convince people to be a Christian, rather than just living before them and speaking who God is to me.

Melody (age 28) Youth Sponsor/Pastor

Evangelism: sharing Christ with others.

Bad Evangelism Story: cold turkey-walked up to two girls in Queen Anne's Hill in Seattle to share salvation with them. I was a part of an evangelism missions project, so the other two members of my team were standing a few feet away praying for me. I asked them if I could ask them some questions (how I was trained). They said, 'OK, if we get to ask you one first.' I agreed. They asked, 'What about evolution?' I said I agreed with the observable science, like survival of the fittest, cause God created it that way to maintain balance/order. So the one girl came back and asked about big bang, and so on. It was more of her wanting to argue/frustrate/confuse me. I couldn't go anywhere further, even if the other girl was open, because this girl was putting up a wall, and their relationship shaped/affected how deep our conversation would go.

Daniel (age 15)

Evangelism: preach.

Good: told someone about God.

Bad: didn't accept it.

Ugly: didn't try again with them.

Ryan (age 15)

Evangelism: bringing people to Christ.

Good: mission trip. We were talking to a guy who talked to us about Jesus. It was awesome!

Bad: guy was high when we talked to him and didn't really care what we were saying.

Rachel (age 12)

Evangelism: when you set an example, like how Jesus would act.

Good: when you help people get to heaven.

Bad: some people don't like the way you tell other people about God.

Haley (age 13)

Evangelism: big word.

Ugly: a priest at a church that I had gone to for the first time informed my six-year-old self that my family would burn in hell . . . yeah.

Tiffany (age 21)

Evangelism: has a negative ring to it for me. I think of people Bible thumping and trying to get people to convert and not really building relationships.

Good: good when done right . . . One way that I have seen work is building a relationship with the person and then opening up conversation about God. This has the power to transform and form lasting friendships . . . the kind of friends that you can call up and ask to pray for you at any time.

Bad: bad is that it seems like when we say we are going to "evangelize," we go out looking for the problems that other people have and try to fix those problems. In other words, we look for the bad in people and try to fix it, rather than looking for the good and using the good to begin dialogue.

Ugly: is when we tear people down and tell them that our "rude" approach is simply the Holy Spirit convicting them of their sins. I think that the ugly side is when we manipulate people into feeling guilty.

Kevin (age 22)

Evangelism: "making disciples."

Good: its sheer focus is on the spread of the gospel message. It is educational in that it does let people know, in creative ways, what people need to know to be "saved."

Bad: it often neglects the physical, mental and emotional needs of the people being reached for their perceived spiritual need. It cares for the soul, but not the body or the mind. Then, if it succeeds in filling the perceived spiritual need, there is often a lack of follow-up to that person so that it can devastate the Christian message.

Ugly: it is too often about the "then and there" without being about the "here and now." People are taught to get through the grub and grime of this life and guarantee their riches in the afterlife. It forgets that eternity starts now and can be enjoyed now. In that light, it often takes a view that sin is fun because it is the way to win here, but if you deny sin, then you will get to have true fun in heaven. But sin is not fun here and now, as it will not be then and there.

Now this is not a scientific sample of people, but it does reflect several common views of evangelism. Most Christians do not think of evangelism as something that is easy or comfortable. Some methods have been effective at one time or in one place, and some methods have been misused or abused. Many have experienced evangelism in both good and bad ways.

It is our hope that this book will help its readers by exploring another method of evangelism—one that is no method at all. This book spends more time talking about the underlying assumptions and foundations beneath evangelism. It's not really new. It focuses on relationship. It is about becoming someone who can easily, comfortably share their faith—without having to become an "evangelist." It is about being a true Christian, whose life is a witness to the love of God. It is about being a true friend, someone who genuinely loves and cares for those around them. With this focus, this book will not tell you how to do evangelism. Instead, it will point you in a direction, and give some helpful advice to get you started. Advice like this: Live for the Kingdom. See the image of God in others. Be a real friend to those around you, and be real with them.

CHAPTER 2
EVANGELISM THROUGH RELATIONSHIP

We have all seen them at one time or another. There on the TV, suit-clad with a Bible in their hand, a preacher asks us to send money so they can organize a rally to spread the "Good News" to people who need to hear it. There is nothing wrong with asking people for money for a worthy cause. And it is our privilege to share the good news about Jesus with people. But haven't you ever wondered about that? First of all, why does it have to take so much money and organization to share about Jesus? Please do not misunderstand, I personally support (financially and otherwise) organizations in other countries that teach people about Jesus. There is a place for organizations like that. But that brings me to my second question—have we fallen into a mindset to send money for someone else to share our faith for us—instead of sharing ourselves? Sure we should send money to support missions—taking the good news of Jesus to places where it has never been, organizing new churches, and reaching out to those who don't know God. It is important to support taking the good news around the world—but what about those people who are near to me? There isn't any need to have some organization collect money to reach my friends and neighbors. *I could reach them.*

Yet I often wonder, what stops us? What keeps us from sharing our faith with our friends? If we know Jesus, if we really believe this Good News that He brings, if we are living in the freedom that salvation offers . . . shouldn't talking to others about our faith happen naturally? So why doesn't it?

Sometimes we feel that we have to be "trained" to tell people about our faith, and be "equipped" properly before doing it. Training can be helpful, but sometimes it makes the whole matter more complicated, and all that training can make us more nervous about sharing. I would like to come to a place where I can easily communicate something that is so fundamental to life: love and relationship. And when you think about it, introducing someone to our closest loved one is not all that complicated. It should come from the same desire we have to run up to our friends and tell them some great news that has happened in our lives. It is sharing a relationship, and in some ways, we do that every day.

The Greek word *euaggelistes,* the word that we translate *evangelist,* literally means "a bringer of good tidings."[2] It is closely related to the Greek word *euaggelion,* the word that we translate as *Gospel* or *Good News.*[3] This idea of *Good News* (and those who bring it) is as old as the Bible itself. There are numerous references to bringing good tidings or good news to others throughout scripture. (One of my favorites is found in Isaiah 52:7, "How lovely on the mountains are the feet of him who brings good news, who announces peace and brings good news of happiness, who announces salvation, and says to Zion, 'Your God reigns!'") However, when we speak about "Good News," we are not simply talking about something that went well that day. This is life-changing news that is for all people who have ever lived! The Good News is that the Creator of everything (God) loves us and desires to be in relationship with us. Moreover, He has made a way for that relationship to happen through the life, death, and resurrection of Jesus Christ, His son. Further, Jesus Christ is actually alive, and through His Spirit we have the power and strength to continue in a right relationship with God. Finally, all of human history is moving toward a final destination. That destination is the return of Jesus and the final consummation of His Kingdom on earth as it is in heaven. In a nutshell, this is the Good News. It is earth-shaking good news about life and eternity. So then, why does it seem that we struggle so much to share this Good News with people we care about? Let's discuss a few possible reasons.

SALES MENTALITY

First, it seems that in all our talk around the church about "equipping" people for evangelism and "training" persons to do it, we have created some expectation that it is not for everyone. Sharing faith must be for those who are gifted "sales people," who could sell ice to penguins. This could not be further from reality! Sharing the Good News, or being an evangelist, ought to be as natural as breathing!

Have you ever bought something on a super-discounted sale price? You get so excited that you call your friend and tell them to get over to the store to buy some too. Of course we would want our friends to know about an outstanding sale. So why do we struggle to tell them about the abundant life and freedom that Christ offers? Because we sometimes think about it as if we are some kind of advertisers or salespeople for God. And deep down we know we are talking about a relationship with Jesus—and we don't want to sound like an advertisement for some close-out item.

All too often, sharing our faith has been made out to be like selling an unwanted product to someone. Have you ever been pressured by a salesperson? Especially the kind of salesperson who was determined to close the deal? I was on the phone the other day attempting to sign up for a new low-interest credit card offer that I had received in the mail. The conversation took quite a bit longer than I had expected; I finally learned that it was better to simply let her talk and not to ask any questions, or the conversation was going to be even longer. At the end of the dialogue, and after all the necessary information had been conveyed, she asked if I would be patient a bit longer to hear about a special program they were offering new customers. I said OK. She then launched into second scripted sales talk for a program which I had absolutely no interest in purchasing. I continued to listen and eat my lunch (I muted the phone so she did not hear me chewing). When she finished, I politely declined the offer. She would not be so easily deterred. She began her attempt to "close the deal" again with a further explanation of how cost-effective it could be for me to purchase this program. When I politely interrupted and told her, "No thanks," she again went back into another approach pattern for the "close." At this point I had now made, finished, and cleaned up my lunch and was ready to head back to work. I interrupted her a second time and explained that I appreciated her time and effort, but I was not going to sign up for this program and was ready to complete the transaction for which I called. She finally gave in and said goodbye. I was glad to finally be off the phone!

When this model of persuasion is the basis for communicating the Good News, it can create an atmosphere of pressure and tension. It can even leave an unfavorable impression by making our friends feel like "customers." In fact, that is likely one of the reasons we don't share the Good News with our friends. We know they are *not* our customers, nor do we want them to be. Since we don't want to appear to be "selling," we feel uncomfortable sharing the Good News. The Good News is not about "selling"; we don't have to approach it as a "product" that we need to persuade someone to "buy."

Expressing our most intimate and important relationship with Jesus Christ with friends ought to flow out of us naturally. Doesn't talking about relationships come up naturally when we are with friends? In fact, I often find myself talking about my good friends when I am around other good friends. It is natural and relaxed, and ought to be. I didn't take any training to learn to tell my good friends about how much I liked other good friends.

PERSONAL PROJECT

I recently came across an advertisement in a Christian magazine that was marketing a "four-week church campaign curriculum."[4] The picture on the one-page ad showed two men who were neighbors. Each had stopped for a conversation while mowing their yards. One of the men had a thought bubble that said, "Shooting the breeze with his neighbor." The other man's thought bubble said, "Laying the foundation for pointing his neighbor to faith."[5] Now, this is likely some wonderful curriculum. And there is a fine line here between an approach to sharing faith that we will be encouraging in this book, and one that we would not encourage. The difference is our attitude.

My only concern about the way of thinking in this advertisement is that it might make our neighbors out to be our personal projects to share Jesus with, rather than living, breathing, intelligent beings who carry the image of God.[6] Frankly, the difference here could be quite subtle, but it is very important. It is one thing to prayerfully expand our circle of friends—as a way of caring for others and intentionally being salt and light in the world. If we don't look to build friendships with those outside of our faith, we could easily be satisfied just spending time with our Christian friends in our own little circle, and never interact with the world at all! So it is good to build relationships outside of that circle. But it is something quite different to see them as projects and not as people—true friends that we care about.

To see someone in any terms less than a child of God, a brother or sister, is to degrade the image of God in them. In our earnest Christian desire to share the Good News, we must be very careful not to begin to see others as projects to be fixed.

TROPHIES OF GOD'S LOVE

Another reason for our evangelism that is similar to seeing people as our personal project is to see them as a trophy to be won. Sometimes we seek to share our faith with others to win them as a way to earn favor with God. We think that we must prove to God that we love Him, or do something to earn His love.

I think we all struggle to trust the fact that God loves and accepts us just as we are. As a result, we work hard to *earn* the love and acceptance which is freely offered. One strange way we try to earn God's love is by doing things for Him that He would never ask us to do: like making our neighbors into a faith sharing accomplishment. Now listen carefully: the motivation for building the relationship is what I am describing here. If a person is only, I repeat *only*, about building a friendship to gain an opportunity to present the Gospel to someone— in my opinion, that is a deception. On the other hand, if we are building a friendship for friendship's sake and then we naturally talk about Jesus because He is the Good News, I think that is how it is meant to work. In the second instance, the two will remain friends regardless of the decision to follow or not follow Jesus. In the first, they may not be friends in either case, because the whole point of the friendship was for the Christian to "do something for God." When we start really loving people simply because they deserve to be loved—because God made them—then we stop seeing them as less than they actually are. We must see them as lovingly created by God for the purpose of relationship with Him.

GIANT HOLES TO BE FILLED WITH OUR MESSAGE

When I was in college, I attended a church with a really good college group. I was still rather young in my faith, so the fact that there were some good-looking college women that attended (about 100 or so) definitely added motivation to get up on Sunday morning (in fact, I ended up marrying one of them about 6 years after college!). The church was quite conservative and even dogmatic in its theological perspective, and that seriously shaped the kind of things the college group participated in. For instance, on Thursday nights in that college town, there was a farmers' market that took over the downtown area. It was a wonderful melting pot of people, entertainment, music, food, and festivities. The college pastor thought it was a perfect place to get a booth and "witness" about Christianity. The way he did it was to invite some of the other college group members who were solid and reasonably knowledgeable Christians to join him to talk to people about their impressions of who God was. They reserved space through the market's organizers and set up a large white board that simply asked, "Who is God?" As people walked by (and usually there were crowds) the students and pastor from the church would politely ask people if they would like to answer the question or hand them a tract (a small pamphlet) about Christianity.

As time went on, this became a significant focus of the college pastor's, and thus the college group's attention. Announcements were made on Sundays inviting anyone to join the group on Thursday nights to "witness" about their faith. There were even testimonials by other college group members about how they were able to share with people that got saved through their conversation. All this time, the pastor was talking more and more about the importance of "winning souls" and what an opportunity we had through this booth. There was also a growing sense in the group that people who really loved God would spend some time downtown Thursday nights witnessing. I was terrified of the idea, but I did love God and felt it was important to prove it to the college pastor, my friends, and God. So, against my better judgment, I signed up.

Luckily for me, that week another member of the small group Bible study, of which I was a part, signed up too. At least I would have a friend. Also to my advantage was the memory verse we were studying that week. It was John 14:6 where Jesus says, "I am the way, and the truth, and the life. No one comes to the Father except through me." My small group prayed for us to have success and I prepared for the coming battle—Thursday night.

When the time finally arrived for me to go, I was incredibly nervous. As I made my way through the dim streets I could smell barbeques and hear the music of several bands. I felt like all eyes were on me as I made my way to the booth. I was greeted by a few of the others that were there and was offered some tracts to hand out. Not really knowing what else to do, I took some and started trying to hand them out to people as they walked by. Some people took the tracts, but most just walked on. Finally someone stopped and wanted to talk. My mouth was immediately dry and my palms sweaty. He saw the white board and shared a genuine thought about who he believed God was. I asked him if he knew Jesus. He said he knew the name and thought Jesus was a good and wise teacher, but nothing more. It occurred to me to share my memory verse, so I did (flawlessly). He basically said "oh" and then politely excused himself. I felt kind of silly. I listened to some of the other conversations that were going on and although most were congenial, one or two were getting sort of heated—like a debate. The pastor joined one, and my small group leader joined the other. The debates continued while I listened in. The pastor and my friend both made good points, shared Scripture, and got their message through. However, neither person chose to pray. I left the booth shortly after to go in search of food.

My friend who led our small group Bible study was fired up! So fired up, it turned out, that he purchased a public address system and started open-air preaching on another corner on Thursday nights. He did this for a while and then started coming to the college campus and doing it there during the time that many students were eating their lunch outside. I heard him a few times, and it was strange—and made me feel strange. He talked a lot about hell and judgment and eternity. He was a lot more forceful, even animated, than he was in normal life. I did not get it. It was like he was acting.

He talked about it more and more at our small group meeting and encouraged each of us to join him. He told us it would prove our love for God. Although I did not have the ability to express then what I can now, I simply explained that it was not for me.

Following those experiences, I felt a mixture of guilt, disillusionment and relief. I felt guilt for not being obedient to spread the Good News. I felt disillusionment that this method of "confronting people with the truth" was talked about as if it were the best way to share our faith, or that it was the only way—or even that it was the main point of Christianity. I felt relief that I had decided not to go back to that church.

After that experience, two very important things happened. First, I found a new fellowship of believers who also earnestly wanted to "spread the Good News," but went about it very differently. They sought to serve people in need and care for the hurting through various service experiences. From serving meals downtown for the homeless, to collecting food for the needy, to visiting people in nursing homes, and visiting other cities to perform service—they spread the Good News about the hope of Jesus Christ without expecting anything in return. Second, and this was truly revolutionary for my life, a guy in the college weight room that I had built a friendship with asked me, "What is it about you?" I had no idea what he was talking about. When I asked for clarity about his question, he said, "I don't know what it is about you . . . you just seem to glow." I was amazed! I had never spoken to him directly about Jesus, but now he was asking me to tell him about Jesus (at least that was the way I saw it, because if I "glowed" it was because of Christ)! I told him very briefly, but very plainly, that I was a follower of Jesus Christ. Giving my life over to Jesus offered freedom from trying to be anything but what you were designed to be by God. I also told him that it was my deepest desire to honor God through the way I lived my life, and that although I had plenty of struggles and temptations, God was faithful to walk with me in an intimately personal way. Admittedly, it was not much, but it was enough. I simply told the truth. My friend's response was kind, respectful, and complementary. He did not pray to receive Jesus as his savior then, and frankly I do not know what happened to him. I do know that we continued to be friends and continued to have mutual respect for each other.

It occurred to me shortly after this that perhaps the best way for me to spread the Good News was to believe it, take it seriously, and allow it to affect every aspect of my life. Perhaps I could trust the Holy Spirit to work in people's lives, and perhaps my responsibility was to be "salt and light"[7] in the world. Interestingly, salt and light do not make any sound. However, they do perform vital functions. Salt preserves, flavors, and seasons. Light shines. This is not to say that I ought never to speak about my faith. But maybe I ought to see people as more than simply receptacles for the message that I want to deliver to them. Maybe they should be respected through mutual friendship, and not characterized as only a soul to be won, or an object for my preaching/witnessing/tract.

GUILT VS. GRACE

Most of us have no problem feeling guilty about things we may have or have not done. In light of this, we have no need for false guilt in our lives. We should never feel guilty about not sharing our faith the exact way someone else does or because someone tells us we ought to. It is our privilege to tell others about Jesus. It is our responsibility to live out our faith and to consider, with growing attentiveness, the daily decisions we make—considering how authentic followers of Jesus Christ should live. I am simple enough to believe that if we actually did that instead of simply going with the flow of the culture (wearing, eating, driving, thinking, listening, speaking what everyone else says and does), then we might really be seen as different. I think it would cause others to ask us why we are different and give us the opportunity to tell them about Jesus. A relationship with Jesus is more than just about life after death. Jesus is about real life, here and now. Real life begins at birth and never ends. Real life is loving God and loving people. Real life with Jesus is not about feeling false guilt, but rather about receiving His grace.

RELATIONAL EVANGELISM

Jesus called His disciples, some who were fishermen, to come and be fishers of men. Fishing is an interesting metaphor. I used to love to fish with my dad. I fished with a simple rod and reel. Some commercial fisherman—like the disciples— fished with nets. It works something like this: they drop large nets down and drag them through the water and then pull them up to see if they caught anything. When there are fish around and they are in the right place at the right time, they might catch some. When there are not, they don't. However, a person with a rod and reel doesn't have the leverage of a wide net to pull off the volume fishing that a net allows. Instead, they have to make the bait look attractive to the fish. One of my favorite ways to fish was trolling. My dad and I would get up early, dress warmly, and go out with hot drinks and food to our little boat that was typically anchored near our campsite. He would help me tie on a "lure" to my pole and put on the proper weights and swivels to get the bait down where the fish were. Then we just motored along slowly, dangling that little shiny metal lure in front of the fish. Every once in a while a fish would bite and, if I was lucky, I would get to reel him in.

I have since come to see the great wisdom of that saying that we can become "fishers of men." Although I am not interested in "catching" anyone, I think the idea of living a life that is attractive to others is applicable here. The real "hook" of sharing the Good News is when the Good News is visible in our own lives. When our lives are characterized by freedom, love, forgiveness, acceptance, service, compassion and grace, people are attracted. It is not that our hair is perfect or we speak flawlessly; rather, that we are authentic, honest, and welcoming. We can be at home in our own skin when we genuinely accept the truth that Christ accepts us as we are—period. When we stop attempting to be what we are not and begin being who we actually are—we become authentic. Then we are being real. That is the type of person I want to be around, and I believe that others feel the same way.

When we begin to live this way, the opportunities to express our faith will come. It may be through an intentional friendship with a neighbor or associate, it may be through an opportunity to serve someone who is struggling, or it may simply be through showing a heart of love and compassion to someone who is in need of a listening ear. The point is not the message as much as it is loving people. When we love God and love our neighbor, Jesus tells us we fulfill the entire Law and Prophets (Matthew 22:37-40). Of course there will be times in our lives when we will need to speak and tell others about Him. But we sometimes forget that we can share our faith just as well if we really focus on loving God with all that we are and expressing that love by loving the people around us. Often that approach can have a more lasting effect on our close relationships than confronting strangers by standing on a street corner with a microphone or in the middle of a large crowd with a sign reminding them to repent or perish.

Of course, the love that I am describing here is much more than a feeling—it is a doing. It is an active love that serves, sweats, listens, and cares; that provides food, time, money, energy, and most of all ourselves to others.

This loving relational sort of evangelism is revolutionary. It is very close to the approach to reaching the world that Jesus took—he built relationships over years with a few close friends, and stayed with them through thick and thin—and the world was changed through them. This approach is alluring, attractive, and magnetic. It does not involve a script, an organized plan, a manual, or confrontations on the street (with or without public address systems). It does not require that you commit anything to memory. It simply involves focusing our entire life on Jesus, and then living in the world. When God becomes our life, then what God loves becomes what we love, and God loves people. So maybe relational evangelism is as much about how we live our whole lives—and how we love—as it is about how we *do* evangelism. Maybe relational evangelism ought to be as natural for followers of Jesus Christ as breathing. Maybe relational evangelism should relieve stress instead of creating it. Maybe relational evangelism ought to be something we do on purpose, every day, and not even realize we are doing it.

CHAPTER 3

IMAGO ME

DISTORTED IMAGO

When I'm on bus trips with students, I like to find out what kind of music everybody else likes. Some students get nervous when I ask to thumb through their CD collections, and others are proud to let me look. Portable media players have allowed us to carry lots of music and watch TV and movies wherever we go. On one of these bus trips, I happened upon a couple of teenage guys who were dually watching a movie on a portable video player. I asked them what they were watching on their itsy-bitsy LCD—it was a horror movie. Not just any horror movie, but a "slasher" movie, based completely upon killing and mutilation. Now as a preteen, I used to think being a teen guy was about three things: pizza, girls, and scary movies. But I was really shocked—maybe because they assumed it was okay to watch it on a youth group bus trip.

After I recovered from my shell-shock and discussed the encounter with a fellow youth worker, I returned back to the guys. My general rule was that if I can hear it, or in this case see it publicly, it falls under my jurisdiction of pastoral domain and discernment. I told them I wanted them to turn it off because this movie objectified people, making them animals or things to be discarded. In so many ways, watching horror movies like this is similar to pornography, in that we infect our minds with images of people that do not depict people as God's creation. We treat them like pieces of meat, instead of beings created in God's image.

They were a little put-off by my speech, but they put the movie away. What really boggled my mind was that we were all returning from a weekend retreat, where we had discussed what it means to be created in God's image, and what it means to see others as created in that image too. We are God's beloved. Being beloved is our identity, and when we treat each other like objects, we deny God's image in others. To become numb to violence and sexuality in entertainment not only diminishes the image of God in others, but rips at the very fabric of who I am as a person.

WHO "I AM"?

Imago Dei (pronounced "im-ah-joe day" or "im-ah-go day") means "image of God." It is the image of God in each of us.[8] God has placed within each person the capacity for deep love for Him and deep godly love for others. In creating and breathing His Spirit into each of us, God's image calls us to a relationship with Him, out of the brokenness of sin. Each person God has created bears His image.

While preparing for a worship gathering and BBQ one Sunday morning in a city park, I had a chance conversation about God's image in us. Hovering on the fringes of our set-up was a guy enjoying the last few drags on his smoke. We struck up a conversation about what we were doing that day, and I welcomed him to join us for lunch. Not sure if he would truly be welcomed, he began to tell me his story. He shared how he was abused as a kid, lived in many big cities and suffered with mental illness. He explained some of his saga as "that's just who I am." Curious, I asked him what he meant by that statement. He said, "Well, you know, I'm gay." Quickly I replied, "Okay, but that's not who you are." He tilted his head in confusion, "What do you mean?"

I replied, "I'm heterosexual . . . but that's not who I am." Even more confused he questioned further, "What?"

"I'm a husband, a daddy, a son, and a pastor, but those titles aren't who I am," I shared playfully. With complete confusion he confessed, "I don't understand."

I said, "Who I am is made in God's image and who you are is made in God's image." Again, my new friend responded with more confusion, "I don't understand that." I would have loved to have kept sharing, but he said he had to go. He had never been told that he was created in God's image and carried that "imago" deep within him. When we begin to realize that we are created in God's image, it helps us to approach every situation welcoming each person we meet as a bearer of God's image. As we see people more and more that way, imagine how it would change how we drive, compete, pay taxes, shop, watch TV, or worship.

GOING DEEP

The most deeply forming retreats I have attended have been "Sabbath" retreats for youth workers. Sponsored by the Youth Ministry and Spirituality Project,[9] these week-long spaces continue to be an oasis in my life. (Have you ever paid for a week of doing nothing with Jesus and complete strangers, and accepting the invitation to rest in your true identity as the beloved of God? Try it. You'll never be the same.)

During one of our morning teachings, a story emerged about a church that was fund-raising for their youth ministry. They were auctioning off students in their youth group for various services to parishioners in order to raise support for an event. What struck me from this common practice was the challenge to examine what we are teaching students about faith when we "commodify" them. My first question was, "What does that mean?"

"Commodify" means to treat a person like they are an object or goods to be traded. That is why we often call these fund-raisers "slave auctions." I'd never heard the words "commoditization" and "youth group" yoked together.

The next question that arose from this discussion was, "Did Jesus commodify people?" The obvious answer is no, and yet He seamlessly shared His Father's love for the people made in His image through the chance encounters on His travels. How did He do that? How do we do that? How can we evangelize (share our faith with) people without commodifying them? This led to all sorts of inquiries. Do I know how to separate the two? How do I share my love for Jesus and the Good News of salvation from self and the brokenness of sin without treating people like an object to be manipulated?

Through a conversation with Michael (the retreat teacher that morning), I began to learn about a world of simplicity—in being and sharing His image. Over coffee, Michael and I discussed the question, "How do I evangelize without turning people into objects?" He explained that when he meets someone, he seeks to be present to him or her in Christ. He lends his identity as the beloved of God to this person, in the simple gift of giving them attention. We become present to God, and through that presence become available to the other person. We allow the deep of who God is in us (*imago Dei*) to become the foundation of what we have to share with them. In this way, the "imago me" (God's image in me) dethrones the selfish "ego" part of me that is seeking to earn God's love. When we seek to serve people from the selfish ego part of ourselves, we end up evangelizing with wrong motives. We turn each person into an "evangelism dollar" with which to buy God's love. But when we recognize the image of God in us, and operate out of that, we find ourselves in a new economy where presence is grace, love is open, and evangelism is a way of "being" in Christ, not something we force on someone. When we remember that we are created in God's image and He loves us, it helps us share our faith with the right motives.

Recognizing the image of God in us also helps us remember that God has already been at work in us—and in our friends. This is called "prevenient grace," ("the grace that goes before us"). It means that God is active in our lives even before we know Him, offering grace and leading us to himself. So God is already at work in the lives of our friends, and when we share our faith, we participate in what God is already doing. We don't have to work to try to save our friends by our evangelism skills, nor do we share in order to make sure God will be pleased with us.

BERATING BRYAN

I recall one particular practice of evangelism. People around us in the dorm were reacting differently to our spiritual awakenings and excitement for God. Some were pumped, some were indifferent, some were confused, and some were frustrated. Bryan was one of the confused. He wasn't really sure where he was or wasn't in this Christ-journey, but I thought I knew for him. If he wholeheartedly didn't know if he believed in Jesus right now, then we (those with Jesus-enthusiasm) needed to fix him—right now! I, and a couple other well-intended souls, kept sharing with Bryan over a three-hour period exactly why he needed to pray to Jesus for forgiveness and invite Him into his heart immediately. After all, his soul was on the line. This should be no problem!

We prayed in our rooms with him, in the stairwell, and finally in a final act of sacred desperation, we convinced him we needed to go pray together in the prayer chapel. Why wouldn't he just give in and get Jesus? All this time there was this nagging thought that falsely assumed any Christian worth their salt could "get somebody" saved—we just hadn't hit upon the right combination to unlock his stubborn heart.

There were some deep-seated issues in his life journey. What he mostly needed were some friends to treat him like a person, a fellow image bearer, and not like a mission to be accomplished. It would have been easy for him to give in just to get us out of his face. He held his confused ground, unsure of all the spiritual hoopla, and was kind to us in the midst of our evangelical endeavors.

We tried to berate Bryan into believing, and it didn't work. I have no idea where Bryan is, or what life has been like, but if I could go back in time, I would have done things very differently.

BACK IN TIME

Suppose I could travel back in time. Suppose I got a "do-over" with how we evangelized Bryan. If I could, I would have chosen to just be available and pray for opportunities for spiritual conversation. I would ask God to draw the people He desired into conversation. I would ask Him to arrange the circumstances and not try to create them on our own. If Bryan had shown interest or curiosity in what was going on, then I would have asked questions and not just given answers. In reflection, the few hours with Bryan were a response to an anxiety deep within me. I worried about my worthiness as a Christian. I questioned how many people I had actually led directly into a saving relationship with Jesus. Looking back I have to wonder, how much of that time with Bryan was about me and my own insecurities, and how much of it was really caring about him and what God was already doing in his life?

God was already present and working. Remember "prevenient grace"? Maybe we missed an amazing opportunity to cooperate with God's Spirit because of our forced-faith tactics. If I could travel back in time, I would choose to be openly available to what God's heart was for Bryan and not assume that I was the key part of Bryan "getting right" with Jesus. I wish I would have trusted in God's Spirit to lead me to share, and give me the words to say. This was an important life decision, not a hard sell for me the salesman.

Our experience with how we came to faith can influence how we think others should come to faith. It can also influence the way we think about God. Think about it. If you came to Jesus through hell-fire and brimstone preaching, you may feel you have to believe in Jesus or else! (You may also wrestle with an unhealthy fear of God and the un-Christ-centered anxiety of snatching souls from the pit of hell single-handedly before Jesus comes storming back.) If you came to faith in Christ through a particular prayer, then you may assume that only those same words are necessary to save your friends. If you came in a loving and patient way, you will naturally employ these methods. If you got hit over the head with the Bible and woke up believing in Jesus, then you'll think everyone should be whacked in the head.

We become very attached to the process by which we came to faith. The danger of this comes in limiting the creativity of the God who created us. He is able to draw people into relationship with Him any way He wants! Jesus said no one comes to the Father except through Him. I believe that. And I believe that the methods and ways He chooses to bring about this grace are already present and active in His Spirit all over creation. We rely on "prevenient grace." This requires a deep trust that God is already at work in the lives of those who have not yet received His invitation. If we desire to share our faith, we would be wise to tune into His Spirit and find out how He wants us to get involved in what He is already doing.

SHARING FAITH IN A COFFEE SHOP

I love coffee, and during my regular visits to my favorite coffee shop, I tried to think of ways to share my faith with one of the clerks who worked there. After several visits of small talk, we started to brave the brim of spiritual conversation. Over the journey of our perforated friendship, I initiated the casual questioning of where she attended church, and her level of involvement. Discovering no affiliation, I invited my "caffeine dealer" to join us for worship whenever I was preaching in the main worship service. I noticed an invisible force field develop following each invitation. I was trying to do a good thing, and she realized it, but politely resisted my attempt to get her inside the doors of our church's facility.

Right about this time, I attended the Sabbath Retreat that I spoke about earlier. I came back with a different perspective.

The next week, I was back to my favorite coffee shop for a caffeine fix—but this time I had a different kind of plan for sharing my faith with the girl behind the counter. This time I would say nothing. The new plan was no plan at all—I would just remain present to God, and in this presence offer the deep of who I am in Christ (imago me) a chance to connect with the depth of how God was already working in the life of my coffee shop friend. I would let Jesus shape the relationship. By the time I reached my second cup, she asked me when I was preaching next. She initiated the conversation toward spiritual things, not me. She was comfortable, open and non-defensive. Wow. What a jump—from plotting out her salvation to recognizing the image of God present in her, and trusting God with her salvation and His love for her.

This approach is not a how-to, but more of an invitation to "be." A step-by-step plan would sort of defeat the purpose. It's an invitation to believe that the image of God is within us, and ruthlessly trust that Jesus wants to bring people to salvation in Him—and that He is involved in the process.

CLAY IS A MESSY ART

Being in Christ can be a messy and imperfect art, but we trust that Jesus is already present, taking the initiative of loving people into His grace. For instance, a friend of mine from my small group had been a PE coach at a middle school for several years and invited me to stop by sometime. That day, dodgeball was the game. When you are in a gym with 100 sixth-graders and complete chaos breaks loose, it's survival of the fittest. The same sixth-grader threw, hit, and caught me out THREE TIMES! One time I threw the ball at him out of complete spite, thinking he wasn't looking. He caught the ball at hip level with a "no-look" skill rarely displayed in any sport.

This PE class was the last period of the day, so my friend and I headed to the parking lot to leave. We stood out front for a while, and students started hanging out and talking. One of the girls from our youth group showed up with clay smeared all over her shirt. She had just exited art class, where a turn on the wheel with a clay project had gone terribly wrong. I asked her if she had any more projects to do in class, and she said she did. I asked if she could make some Communion cups for our youth group. Having never thought about that, she was a little stunned and immediately called a friend over whose skills she said were amazing. Her friend asked me if I wanted turned or spiral cups. I said I liked little bowls like what may have actually been at the Passover meal[10] of the Last Supper. She agreed that she would work on them.

Why did I bother to include this story? It opens up possibilities for spiritual conversations with our friends—but in a gentle way. How cool would it be for this student to be molding these cups and explain to her teacher and friends why she chose this project for class? The story of Christ comes gently into the public domain with a subtle, yet powerful, message of hope and love. Six simple cups that represent the salvation of the world. An ordinary conversation in front of an ordinary middle school, and it opens up the possibility of a relationship turned into emerging faith.

The story of God's invitation to humanity sneaks on the scene once again. I like that. That's what *imago Dei* is all about. God's image is in us. We are becoming who Christ is calling us to be and we let God be who He wants to be in us.

Evangelism is the work of the Spirit moving in the lives of people around us. Through His grace, God is moving people toward himself. A life lived in love (one that is built on the foundation of knowing that they are created in God's own image) is often the catalyst that is used by God to start this process. This process is the beginning of a journey toward salvation through Jesus Christ.

CHAPTER 4
IMAGO YOU

A STORY OF BEING RELATIONAL

Seeing the image of God in ourselves is the beginning of seeing the image of God in others. How do we really begin to recognize, validate, and embrace the image of God in others—*actually love them*—and in this way fulfill "all the Law and Prophets?"[11] It is one thing to love the people we know, friends and family;[12] it is another to love the people with whom we only occasionally interact. Let's explore what it might look like in an everyday life.

The first time I interacted with John was on my phone. I was sitting behind his truck and large cargo trailer, waiting for the light to change. When he turned before me, I noticed that his trailer was advertising his "Mobile Lube" business. I was intrigued. It appeared from its name that he would come to your house or work to change the oil in your car. Although I figured the price for that kind of service would be cost prohibitive for me, when I got home I dialed the seven large digits stenciled on his trailer wall. He didn't answer, so I left a message.

I heard back from John a short time later. We talked about his business and the price he charged to come to his customers for an oil change. Although it was not low-priced, he explained that he also filled up all fluids in the car and even made sure the tires were properly inflated. That sounded like a good value to me. We agreed that he would come to my house that Saturday, and we said our goodbyes.

John showed up on a beautiful, spring morning. We talked a bit, and I explained how I had seen his trailer on the road, and he asked if I would like see the inside of it. I told him I did. It was amazing! He had it all rigged up to deal with used oil; it also had electric pumps attached to filler hoses in several different bins for filling up radiator fluid, brake fluid, automatic transmission fluid, windshield wiper fluid, and oil. We talked for several minutes about how he got started in this business and how it had grown over the years. He was obviously a creative, intelligent, and hard-working business man.

When he finished the service on my car, he came to the door and knocked. He handed me a professional-looking slip of paper that listed all the work he had done. I invited him in and wrote out a check for the service. We talked for a few more minutes. I introduced my wife and son, and then he excused himself for his next appointment. That is how it all began.

For the next two or three years, I called upon John to come to our house or my office to change the oil in our cars. He was always faithful to come and always expressed appreciation for the business. I was often struck by his humble servant heart and gentle spirit. Our conversations grew in length over this time. I started to gather bits of information about his life and was able to ask him about things he talked about the last time we were together. I came to see John as an utterly unique and exquisite creation of God. He had so many admirable qualities, and I was delighted to call him my friend. Then it happened.

John's elderly mother was in a car accident. John was at our house to change our oil about two weeks after it happened. As we exchanged the usual pleasantries between friends, I asked him how things were at the farm. (John lived on a plot of 200 acres with his mother. They sort of took care of each other.) For the first time since I'd known him, John answered, "Not too good." He explained that his mother had been hit by a car that had failed to yield at a stop sign. She was pretty seriously injured, and the doctors were particularly concerned about her head, neck, and back. John went on to explain that his mom was in the hospital in Salt Lake City, where specialists were taking care of her. I began praying for her and for John, even while I listened to him.

John was obviously shaken. He told both Sandy and me about how his father had died a few years ago, and that was when John moved back home to be with his mom. He missed his dad and had never considered that his mom would have health issues any time soon. She was getting older, but was very active and healthy. I assured John that we would pray for them in the coming weeks, and would trust God to bring healing to her and peace to him. It was the first time we had talked overtly about faith, God, or anything related to religion. Of course, he knew I taught at a Christian university and that we attended church, but not much more beyond that had been shared. He expressed sincere gratitude for my offer and assured me that it was a comfort to know that people besides his family were supporting him. With that, he set off to service our car. When he finished, he again expressed thanks for our support and I assured him we were already praying for him and his family.

Frankly, I expected things to go well for him and his mom. She sounded like she was quite healthy and would likely make a full recovery. Unfortunately, that was not what transpired.

It was a hot, summer afternoon the next time we saw John. We were putting sprinklers in, and John met us in the backyard.

One of the first things I asked him was how his mom was doing. He paused, and seemed to get choked up a bit. She had just recently died. Sandy and I were in disbelief! How could this have happened? We dropped our tools and quickly walked to his side to put reassuring hands on our friend and brother. I began to silently pray. He did not break down in sobs—although I felt like I could for him. He explained how the specialists were so concerned about her spine that they missed the damage to her internal organs. When her neck and spine were reasonably healthy, they allowed her to go home. Just a couple days after returning to the farm, she complained a bit about pain in her stomach—she never talked about pain, according to John—and a day later, she died in the emergency room. John was shocked. He seemed so fragile. I simply stood with my hand on his shoulder and listened to him continue his attempt to make sense of these recent events.

I asked if he had a supportive community of people around him to help, like a tight group of friends or a church. He told me that people at the church his mom attended were faithfully looking in on him. I did not ask John to come to our church, but encouraged him to not be alone. I think we can trust the Holy Spirit to reach through any situation to those in need and reveal the truth of Christ to them. In fact, Psalm 34:18 assures us that, "The LORD is close to the brokenhearted and saves those who are crushed in spirit." This described John perfectly. He explained how his sister and brother had come to stay for a while. I told him how important that was, to feel the support of others at times like this, and said we would like to do anything we could that might be helpful for him too. I assured him our prayers would continue for him, and encouraged him to express his emotions to God, too. I told him that God can handle all the feelings he was experiencing. He is a big God and is not offended by our genuine expressions of anger, grief, frustration, and the like. We must have talked in the hot sun for 45 minutes or so.

We did not really do anything for John that day in physical, measurable terms, but we listened and mourned with him. In doing this very small act, we validated his humanity. It was not pity we showed, but rather empathy. The two are very different. We stepped into his suffering and hurt with him. In this way, we recognized and embraced that John was a child of our God and that God's image was in him. It was not about which church he had once attended or what his theological understanding was. This was much larger. What was the most important thing in these moments was not to get John to repeat some prayer of "forgiveness," but rather to allow the God of all comfort, who has comforted us, to comfort John through us.[13] The most important act we could do in these moments was to listen to John. Through listening and giving John our time and attention, we were giving ourselves to John. What else is more precious and personal to us than our time? We were recognizing the truth of Matthew 25:40, where Jesus says, "Whatever you did for one of the least of these brothers of mine, you did for me." In being fully present to John in his need, we were identifying God's image in John and authenticating that image. When we move quickly past people in need on the street or wherever, we move quickly past the God who identifies with the lowly and needy in His world. It is part of the human condition to want to be recognized and related to on equal terms, not to feel that others are bending down to your level due to your need. We attempted to do this with our friend John at this difficult moment in his life.

We finished talking and I invited him to join us for dinner in the near future. He paused, looked me square in the eyes, and said that he would really enjoy that. He then turned and set off to work.

It was a few weeks before John came to our home for dinner. But once he was there, we were able to express the genuine love of Christ through our hospitality. My wife is an exceptional cook, and to come to our house for one of her meals means you are in for a treat. This is the way we chose to love and comfort our friend John. Sharing our bread and drink with another is one of the most fundamental and personal ways to say to another person, "You matter to me."

We talked about many things that night. We talked about John's business, the farm, his mom, church, death, life, and prayer. It had been several weeks since the funeral, but it was all still very fresh for John. John mentioned he had been doing some praying and was sensing the comfort of God in his life.

At the end of the evening, as I poured him a second cup of decaf, we continued to talk and eat dessert, and in this way share in communion together. In fact, the entire evening had been an act of community or communion. Our house is dedicated to Jesus, our children have been baptized and dedicated to Jesus, our lives are dedicated to Jesus, and when we thanked God for the meal that evening, we again invited Jesus to be the unseen guest at the table. I like to think that John saw Jesus that evening in our home, in our kids who sat on John's lap, in the meal that was lovingly prepared by my godly wife, in our genuine interest in him and his life, and even in me—a fellow journeyer on this path that we call life.

John expressed tremendous gratitude that evening for the invitation. However, the story is not over with John. I do hope to talk explicitly about Jesus Christ with him someday. But I did not want to create a situation where, with him in our home for the first time, eating our food and sitting at our table, he was "forced" to listen to me discuss my faith just so he could eat with us. Some would argue that I missed a golden opportunity. I would argue that we can trust the Holy Spirit to communicate with people in words that are not spoken aloud. And further, I trust that God loves, cares for, and is at work in John's life already. You see, John is my friend. He is not my project, an object for me to "win" for God, or anything other than an individual for whom I have great respect, and whom I genuinely like. It is very clear to John where we stand in our faith. He has been in our home now on several occasions and knows how we conduct our lives, and how we treat our kids. He has witnessed the deep love that my wife and I share. He has heard me pray to Jesus Christ, and has been a part of those prayers. He has sat at our table as we invited God's blessing on our meal. John knows about God from his mom. John knows about God from his church. John knows about God because God is at work in his life (and everyone else's) already. My part is to be faithful to live my life dedicated to God, to love people, and to allow God to lead us to a time to share openly about our faith.

RELATIONAL EVANGELISM

What I have just described could be called "relational evangelism." Relational evangelism is not a program, but a way of living. It is simply about being completely sold out to God—then accepting the invitation to share life with people that God brings across your path. One of those people in my life is John, and I am seeking to be faithful.

Relational evangelism is an intentional way of living. It is linked with being a missionary more than anything else. In other words, we see ourselves as missionaries to our own culture. (It is the idea behind the early Christian hymn recorded in Philippians 2:5-11.) The cultures in North America are heavily "spiritual,"[14] but often far from Christian. As a result, there are innumerable opportunities daily to step into the gap in people's lives as an example of Jesus Christ.

REACHING OUT TO THOSE AROUND US

To illustrate, let me share a story about a person who did this at my high school. Her name was Jen. I met her my freshman year and she made a difference in my life for Jesus Christ. In fact, it was Jen who first introduced me to relational evangelism, and what it might look like for Jesus to be a high school student. You see, Jen was the type of person that was kind to everyone. She was relatively popular, athletic, and adventurous. Jen was the kind of friend that everyone wanted. She did not gossip (imagine that!) and was loyal and reliable. She was a fairly good student, but not a total brain.

What made Jen's faith stand out so brightly was the way she dealt with the social part of high school life. Jen was always where people were. If it was a huge party, Jen was there—but not drinking alcohol. Instead, she did what she could to help those who were drunk, sick, or threatening to fight. If it was a dance, Jen was there having a great time, but she never went to a hotel room with a guy when it was over, and her dates always understood that. If it was a sporting event like a football game, Jen was there dressed in school colors, screaming her lungs out for our team, but also keeping her head about her if we lost. If it was a day at the beach—like senior skip day—Jen was there with her parents' permission and knowledge, and characteristically watching out for those of us who had tendencies to do stupid things without parents around.

Jen was sort of a guardian angel for the high school. No one assigned her that task. She just took it on. Because of her close relationship with Jesus Christ, she had a deep and caring heart. She just could not help wanting to reach out to those in need. If my high school years were at all representative, then there are lots of needs in the lives of high school students. Jen was often there, encouraging us to think through what we were considering, or helping us pick up the pieces afterward.

I will never forget her and the impression she left on my life. She was a committed Christian and was happy to talk to you about her faith, but she never "preached" at anyone, including me. She just lived a devoted life to Jesus in our high school and we all knew what she was about. (She lived in stark contrast to another Christian student who carried his Bible to class and told many of us we were sinners and likely not going to make it to heaven if we did not change our lives. He was right, but the way he went about sharing the Good News was just so *in your face*, and mostly rejected by those who listened. I'm sure there are some who responded to his message, and God has worked through that approach in the past, but I was not one of those who responded to it. His method pushed me away.)

It was our senior year, and graduation was just a couple weeks away. I had the opportunity to go out to lunch with Jen, to sort of say goodbye and to thank her for her faithful friendship over the past four years. We went out to a local burger place and had a fun time talking and reminiscing about places we had been and things that had happened over the last four years. We stood amazed that it was all coming to an end and that our paths may never cross again. It was a sort of bittersweet realization.

Jen knew all about me. She knew that I struggled with sexual promiscuity, in spite of the fact that I had made a commitment to Jesus as a small boy. She saw through my so-called "success" in high school—I was fairly popular, team captain, homecoming king, and so on. She also knew that I was not really happy, and that I had a deep longing for something more. She knew that longing was for Jesus, and that I would never have true joy without Him. Although I had done some pretty sinful things in high school, Jen never judged me and was always my friend.

As I drove back in the school lot, Jen looked at me intently just before we got out of the car. I noticed her look and said, "What?" She looked at me and asked, "When are you going to take Jesus seriously?" The question penetrated the deepest part of me. It was as if God himself was asking. I did not answer her, but I told God that I would start that very moment.

We had talked about Jesus, the Bible, and Jen's faith before, but never in four years had she been so direct with me. And this is important—she *could* be direct with me, because she was my friend. Jen had earned my deepest respect by the way she lived her life and how she treated me, even though I had not always treated her as well. And now she was speaking out of all of those years she had invested in me. She asked me to make a decision for Jesus—and I did.

We got out of the car and went our separate ways. I did tell her before that school year was over about the decision I made. She was shocked. I told her I was not going to sleep around anymore, that I was going to read my Bible and go to church. I kept those promises.

The remarkable thing about Jen was that she saw the image of God in people, and treated them with the respect and dignity warranted by the image of God in them. Even when a person's actions did not deserve it, Jen did not treat them differently. She saw the image of God in me, in spite of the bad things I did. She was the first relational evangelist I ever knew. Her life was her sermon, and her friendship was her gift.

I like to think that Jen discovered early in life an important idea regarding sharing our faith: when we recognize God's image in others and treat them accordingly, then we can commune with God in our everyday interaction with people. Please do not misunderstand what I am saying. There are not little bits of God in every person, but in each person there is a representation of the Creator himself. It is like seeing the creation of a great painter or sculptor like Michelangelo. I have had the privilege of traveling to Italy and seeing many of Michelangelo's works—the Sistine Chapel in Rome, and the great statue of David that stands in Florence. Although I am not a connoisseur of art, when I saw these truly remarkable creations, I experienced the brilliance of a man born over 500 years ago. It was not the man himself that I saw—Michelangelo physically in the works of art, but a representation of his heart, mind, and passion left an image of himself on those works. He had contributed something that was utterly personal to the marble and the plaster through his carving and painting.

In a similar way, God leaves His image in and on and through us, because of His work in creating us. (He restores His image in us by redeeming us.) There is an utterly personal mark on each person. That mark is from God himself. So in the same way that we are able to "see" Michelangelo through his artwork, we can "see" God through recognizing His image in others. As we interact with others throughout our day, it is not unlike walking through various works of art, all produced by a profoundly personal creator who has left an impression of himself on each of us.

There is a quote attributed to Michelangelo regarding his approach to carving the large marble blocks from which his most famous statues came. It states, "I saw the angel in the marble and carved until I set him free."[15] You see, he did not make the marble what he wanted it to be; instead he looked at the marble until he was able to discern what was already there, and then removed all that was disabling the world from seeing its beauty. Many of our brothers and sisters in this world are trapped inside broken lives, bodies, situations, families, and so on. They are trapped, and their beauty of being made in God's image is "marbled over," even to themselves. When we treat others with the respect, compassion, and authenticity that they deserve as a creature carrying the image of God, we take a small piece of marble away that helps to reveal their beauty to the rest of the world. When we offer authentic friendship and our very personal selves to others, we act as sculptors illuminating the works of art that people are—not only to themselves, but to all of creation.

Join us in recognizing and revealing the image of God in everyone we meet.

CHAPTER 5
KINGDOM COME

COFFEE TALK

This chapter is dangerous because it's not filled with answers. Questions dwell here. It's an invitation to create, to question, to seek, and to find. It's an invitation to being the church that Christ intended, and living out the kingdom of God. It's an old invitation, not a new one. We are not looking to be right or wrong, but I'm wondering if there are some things going on that we've been missing in the life of the church and Kingdom. Maybe there are some questions here that need to be asked.

I'm a coffee shop theologian. I'm not an accomplished scholar, or outstanding in the field of anything. I'm an everyday guy who loves to grapple with the essence of faith. There's something to this Kingdom stuff. Jesus spoke of it a lot—pointing to the Kingdom. He told people they are near to it, or far away from it. He rarely gave specifics of what the Kingdom actually is. What if, instead of trying to explain all of that and trying to know all the answers, I just ask several questions regarding the Kingdom and the church?

Can you be in the Kingdom and not in a church?

Can you be in a church and not in the Kingdom?

What's the difference between going to church and living out the Kingdom?

THE KINGDOM NOW

We sell short the prayer of Jesus regarding the Kingdom coming (Matthew 6:10 and Luke 11:2) when we don't talk about salvation as something we experience now, and reduce it to a heaven and hell thing. Salvation is more than just deciding that we don't want to go to hell and do want to go to heaven. It involves a change to the center of life. Life becomes centered in the kingdom of God. All that we do and all that we are become centered around living as subjects of the King of Kings, Jesus Christ. Salvation is very much about the here and now. It is about living in the joy of the kingdom of God which is breaking in upon the earth. It is receiving and participating in seeing the will of our King done here "on earth, as it is in heaven." (Matthew 6:10). It impacts everything we are and do—including church.

WHAT IS THE CHURCH?

I love singing, teaching, prayer, discussion, and communion together. This is all part of church, but it's not all there is to being the Church. As I sat in our amazing main worship service the other day looking at the back of heads, I thought about how being the church is so much more than what we make it out to be. I completely believe we should gather together as believers in Christ. That's one of the meanings of the word "church"—to gather. But sometimes we change the gathering into something else. In our rituals and routines, *doing* church becomes something different from *being* church.

So we have to ask ourselves, what is the church? What are we doing, and what are we supposed to be?

At best, the church on earth and the kingdom of God become the same thing. When we are living out all that it means to be the church, then we are living out all that it means to be a part of the Kingdom, and vice versa.

But we have been living with the word "church" for so long, and doing church in certain ways for so long, that we sometimes don't see when the two don't match up. Church is visible—we can see the building, we see each other when we gather together. We recognize that there are meetings and gatherings and events, and we can call all of those things "church." But it is very easy to fall into a trap of just doing what everyone else is doing, and doing what we see the world doing—and still calling it church.

For example, our churches can very quickly start looking like and operating like the businesses in which our members work the other six days of the week. We bring that business model with us into church life. This has a significant impact on the way we think about church. We start to think of our pastor as the CEO. Both kinds of organizations have a "board of directors." We go to church like we go to work—when our work day is done, we go home to relax and leave it behind—and pretty soon we start thinking about church that way. At work, when we need to get a job done, we form a committee, or we bring it to our boss, or we outsource it to some other company. Sometimes the work is ours, but we have very clearly defined ideas of what work is ours to do. If something comes our way that we are not trained in or comfortable with, we quickly say, "That's not my job." If we start thinking of church that way, then our outreach becomes a job. We don't see ourselves as the ones qualified to share our faith, so instead we will invite our friends to come to church—that is where the work gets done. We have highly trained workers there, and we can hand off evangelism to their department. Essentially, we get someone else to do our job for us.

Kingdom thinking is never like that. The whole idea of "kingdom" is a realm where we live. We cannot leave it back at the office. We are subjects of the King, wherever we go, whatever we do. The Kingdom is all around us—in fact, Jesus said the kingdom of God is *within us* (Luke 17:21). It is a part of us. We carry it inside of us everywhere we go—at work, at home, at church. So when we think in terms of the Kingdom, it is much more difficult to misunderstand or mistake it for something else. The business model does not work in the Kingdom, because there is no CEO—there is one king over everything, and that is Christ. It is much more difficult to think about the Kingdom in terms of a building or meetings. The Kingdom is a part of us. It is like being a part of a realm—we all live in this realm and it is around us (and within us) all the time.

As subjects of this realm, we receive all the benefits that come from our King. We receive His peace. We have His provision—He takes care of all of our needs. We become children of the King, and so we know His love and kindness. We also become His heirs—we will inherit this Kingdom (Luke 12:32).

So when we think about evangelism and sharing our faith in Kingdom terms, we can approach it differently. Evangelism viewed through Kingdom lenses looks less like a job to be done and more a natural part of who we are. It is a part of being subjects of this realm. For example, when we meet someone, we treat them with hospitality, like when someone comes to visit our country. We give them directions if they don't know the way around. We might even take them around and show them the sights. We would happily tell them about our King and life in this realm.

BEING A CATALYST

Seeing the Kingdom in this way has made me look at church differently. Maybe the church's role is to be a catalyst for the Kingdom come. I learned enough in chemistry class to learn the definition of a catalyst. It is something that causes a reaction, and makes something happen. (Like when you drop a dissolving tablet in water.) I knew enough about chemistry to know if you start dumping chemicals together, eventually something is going to happen. When a new substance is added to an existing substance, and something happens, the added substance is called a *catalyst*.

Have you ever heard that to remove the grime build-up around your toilet bowl you could use ALKA-SELTZER? I was desperate—so I tried it. I plopped the round little catalyst tablets into the water with a splash and immediately the fizzing began. Then it disappeared. "That didn't work," I said to myself. Sometimes we act like this as a church: "Jesus, just let us fizz a little in the world and then take us away." Yet, it seems that the way that Jesus lived His life involved being a continuous reaction in the world. Jesus wants us to be the kind of catalyst that is continually making things happen—Kingdom things. The church is one of the ways that God designed for His Kingdom to come—it is a way that His will is done on earth—through us, the church.

PLAY IN SUCH A WAY . . .

One dilemma churches face involves competitive Christian sports. How do we play nice while seeking to win? Competitions can bring to the surface attitudes and actions that we, and the folks around us, never knew we were capable of!

We have some students in our youth ministry that love to play dodgeball. As we were preparing for a competition with other churches, I realized that it might be good to have a conversation about what it meant to compete in a Christ-centered way. In preparation, I talked with my friend Bob, who had lots of coaching and competitive experience but always sought to live like Jesus in the process. He gave me some good advice: challenge our students to play in such a way that the other teams are glad they played us. It took some conversation and reminding, but our youth played their hearts out and had a blast. It seemed like the other teams did enjoy playing dodgeball with us.

What if we lived as the church in such a way that other people were glad they knew us?

What if instead of proclaiming Jesus on the street corners, people who had no idea about Jesus began praising and worshipping God in the streets because they knew us? What if we lived in such a way that everyone we knew experienced Jesus, who is "God with us," because they somehow experienced God by being "with us"? This would happen not because of how amazing we are, but because of the amazing Spirit of God that lives within us. When we are living as His body on earth, His Church becomes a catalyst for His Kingdom. What if God's kingdom means His dreams for the redemption of creation (Romans 8:20-22) are coming true? What if it means restored relationship with humanity, people accepting God's offer for relationship through Jesus' saving sacrifice on the Cross? What if the role of the church is to seek what God is doing, and then participate in it?

Jesus lived out the kingdom of God before the world. That's

the role of the church—living out the Kingdom. The kingdom of God is in many ways God's dreams for us coming true through His relationship with humanity.

We can hide in a large gathering. We can get by, get lazy, critique, and be satisfied with consuming. Being the church is more than a once-a-week event. It is more than songs, preaching, and how we dress. It is more than something we are required, obligated, supposed to, or have to do. Church is living. Church is dynamic and active. Being the church is an adventure. I believe the church is intended to be a catalyst for the kingdom of God.

Jesus was calling people into the Kingdom. He calls the church, the people that make up His Body in belief, to live out the Kingdom. Maybe we need to re-imagine what it means to be the church?

RE-IMAGINING CHURCH

I was watching an episode of SpongeBob Squarepants, where Patrick and SpongeBob were playing in a giant box—the most exciting noises were coming from this box. They made it sound like they were really rocketing through space or on a pirate ship. It was so real to them. It was so real to them that their neighbor, Squidward, was frustrated at all the racket they were creating inside their box. He couldn't figure out how two goofballs like Patrick and SpongeBob could be having so much fun inside an ordinary box.

When they weren't looking, Squidward climbed in the box and saw exactly what he'd expected—nothing but a plain old box. There was no excitement, joy, or danger like he had heard his friends experience together.

Patrick and SpongeBob were playing in the box again the next day. Again, Squidward became frustrated. What could possibly be so good about the box? That was when Squidward learned the secret of the box—the secret that let SpongeBob and Patrick be astronauts or pirates at their whim: *imagination.* Imagination made it all come alive.

Sometimes it's not about getting out of the box or getting a new box, it's about using our imagination inside the box—re-imagining.

We are at a crucial stage in the history of being the church. We need to re-imagine inside the boxes of our traditions and rediscover what it means to be the church. We need to look, taste, touch, smell, and imagine with the creativity of the Creator, whose image we bear.

Instead of leaving our churches out of frustration, or not attending when we see that our churches are not perfect, let's re-imagine what God's desire is for His Bride. How do we imagine ourselves as His witnesses—lights to the world? Is it possible to imagine sharing our faith by living out the Kingdom in all of our relationships—and prayerfully sharing with them as the Spirit leads us? Let's join God in what He dreams to do inside His body. Let's re-imagine being the church.

WHAT IS THE KINGDOM?

Jesus didn't come to start another religion. He came to show us how to be with one another in the chaos of a fallen world—to advance the coming of His Kingdom.

Maybe the church should be a catalyst for the Kingdom. The church should be causing a reaction in the world because of the life of Christ in us, and people should be coming into the Kingdom because of this Christ-reaction.

If a catalyst is a reaction when two chemicals come into contact, then church and evangelism in some way should be about bringing our relationships into contact with Jesus Christ. When the Kingdom advances, it is because new relationships with Christ have formed from these contacts. In some ways, the Kingdom is a way of relating.

The kingdom of God is not a geographical destination, but a relational process. The Kingdom breaks in upon the earth when God's dreams for humanity come true in the world. Jesus was always pointing out the Kingdom. In Luke 17:20-37, He reveals the Kingdom is in us. If the Kingdom is in us, then maybe that has something to do with the image of God—we carry God's kingdom in us just as we are formed in His image. Maybe those abandoning their lives to God in Jesus' name (the Church) practice the Kingdom when they interact with their world.

RELATING IN THE KINGDOM

You know the conversation Jesus had with the guy who asked him which was the greatest commandment (Matthew 22:34-40, Mark 12:29-31)? Jesus hangs everything on loving God with all you are, and loving your neighbor as yourself. The greatest commands are all about relationship—all about how we relate to God and how we relate to each other. They're about giving ourselves fully to the Creator and recognizing that God created and loves those around us.

The beginning of Kingdom relationships is the practice of recognizing each person as someone who is created in the image of God. In many ways our relationships at their best are the image of God in me recognizing the image of God in you.

67

Dietrich Bonhoeffer implies in his book, *Life Together*, that it's never just you and me. The way we relate is always me and you and Jesus.[16] Not three separate entities, but three connected ones.

Relationships in the Kingdom transcend race, religion, creed, doctrine, and culture. Jesus came to proclaim that God's Kingdom has come—and has brought to us a way of relating that trumps every other way of relating.

God invites us to be a catalyst for the Kingdom come—His will being done on earth as it is in heaven. God can make it happen without us, but I think He really wants to be in relationship with His Church—His Bride. And part of that means building relationships—with God and with each other, with those in the church and those outside of the church. In this way, we become a catalyst for others entering His Kingdom. Let's take a chance and allow God's Spirit to work through us. And as the church seeks Kingdom, we will discover what being the church really means.

As we live this Kingdom life, we join something that God has always been doing. He's always been about welcoming the straggler in, and calling out to His creation to come back to relationship with Him.

A KINGDOM PEOPLE

The other day I was at the park with my son and we saw a man with his metal detector. He was waving it methodically over the ground, waiting to hear the "beep" that signaled possible buried treasure. In conversation, I discovered this man had found hundreds of watches and rings—even diamond rings. I asked him if he ever got money for them. He said, "No, I keep them in a big drawer." He liked to get them out and look at them. I asked if he ever got them appraised. He said, "Yes, just to see if the diamonds are real." He never sold them. Bottom line: he had a valuable stash of stuff and he liked to look at it.

Do we do this with life in Christ, the church, and Kingdom? We have valuable treasure we just put in storage and never share. Becoming Kingdom people is about sharing the Good News of the love of God. It's the treasure of Jesus' love in the world that changes things, and it has the power to transform lives.

We can choose to hoard the blessing of God's love that we have received. We can make church into a corporation, where we reduce people to products to be counted. We can focus all our attention on the church building, or on all of the events that fill our schedules. We can make the church into a country club where we have memberships and there are "insiders" and "outsiders" and the two don't mix. Or we can let the Spirit make our church life into a catalyst for Kingdom relationships.

As God's Kingdom people, we begin to think in Kingdom terms. We see the image of God in each person, and see how much God loves them and wants them to be a part of His Kingdom. We see how God wants to provide for them and care for them in His realm. We begin to see those around us as fellow travelers on a journey toward God, and we befriend them and help them on their way.

Evangelism is no longer something to be worried about. It becomes a part of our lifestyle—the lifestyle of God's Kingdom people. It is simply being a friend, and as the opportunities arise, sharing with them about the love of the King. That is what it means to live out this Kingdom, and what it means to be the church.

"The Church gets in trouble whenever it thinks it is in the church business rather than the Kingdom business. In the church business, people are concerned with church activities, religious behavior, and spiritual things. In the Kingdom business, people are concerned with Kingdom activities, all human behavior, and everything God has made, visible and invisible. Kingdom people see human affairs as saturated with spiritual meaning and Kingdom significance. Kingdom people seek first the Kingdom of God and its justice; church people often put church work above concerns of justice, mercy and truth. Church people think about how to get people into the church; Kingdom people think about how to get the church into the world. Church people worry that the world might change the Church; Kingdom people work to see the church change the world . . . If the church has one great need, it is this: To be set free for the Kingdom of God, to be liberated from itself as it has become in order to be itself as God intends. The church must be freed to participate fully in the economy of God."

—Howard A Snyder,
Liberating the Church: The Ecology of Church and Kingdom, P. 11.

"Seek first His kingdom and his righteousness." (Matthew 6:33).

CHAPTER 6
A STORY FROM THE ROAD

MY FRIEND TIM[17]

I met him right after the first Sunday morning service. He made his way down toward me at the front of the sanctuary as soon as the last "Amen" was said. He looked as if he could have ridden with the Hells Angels motorcycle gang. (I later learned that he had.) He was a bit over 6 feet tall, sported a shaved head, tattoos, big black combat boots, sunglasses, worn jeans, white t-shirt, and a long Fu Manchu mustache. He was very animated when he introduced himself, and immediately began asking me about the prayer I had led during the service. He wanted to know if I had written the prayer out beforehand, or if I just "made up" the words on the spot. I smiled, sort of chuckled, and told him they were my own words that had simply come from my heart. Tim was genuinely intrigued by that. He couldn't seem to wrap his mind around the fact that my 5-7 minute sort of prayer monologue had not been thought out beforehand. I immediately liked Tim. He was sort of childlike. He was this big, approachable sort of person who was genuinely interested in whether I had read or actually had a "live" conversation with God!

What struck me the most about my conversation with Tim that morning was my awareness that he would very likely not last too long at my church. It was pretty obvious from the way he dressed and carried himself that he didn't "fit" there. Now, please do not misunderstand what I am intending to say; it is not that he was not welcome. But the clothes he wore, the language he used, and the car he drove were not those sported by the majority of the highly-educated, middle-class congregation. I had seen people like Tim come to our church before, and it wasn't but a few weeks or months later that they had disappeared—never to return. Someone may have even followed up on them, but they weren't coming back—they just did not fit. It is one of the very real and often sad realities of the human condition that people typically congregate with people of similar status (similar income level, social groups, etc.). It was clear that this was not his crowd, and although Tim was more than welcome to attend our church, in a few weeks or months he would stop. At least, that is what I thought—obviously I did not know Tim!

Not only did Tim continue to come to our church, but in the coming weeks, he began bringing his girlfriend (who was pregnant with Tim's child), his son (from another woman), and any kids from the neighborhood that wanted to come. Further, as our relationship continued to grow, he asked me if he could sit up in the front row with my wife and me. I invited him to join us anytime.

The next week, and every week after that, Tim was at church. He sat in the front row with my wife and me. Even better than all that, Tim and his "crew" would often arrive after the service had started. As a result, the three or four of them would enter the back of the sanctuary and make their way all the way down to the front and noisily sit down next to us. Tim had a distinct limp too, which just added to the "production" of them coming down the aisle. When he arrived at our row, there would be the typical pleasantries of us each greeting the other and, in time, even hugs. This would, of course, cause a bit of an interruption, but after my initial embarrassment with these regular entrances, I realized that if Jesus himself were in the service, He would likely show the same, if not much more, genuine excitement at their presence and even celebration at their desire to be "front and center" in church. So what if it caused a bit of a commotion? Is it not the Sabbath for humanity and not humanity for the Sabbath?[18] Would it not be appropriate to give attention to an individual who carries the image of God as they enter this house of worship—over listening to the announcements? It is not that I am advocating for us to ever be "disrespectful" during a worship service, but I had come to learn from Tim that coming to church was something new for him, as was any sort of "organized" religion. I felt that the occasion warranted a mini-celebration each time he chose to come into God's house to lift up His name. So I chose to welcome him with open arms each time he came, in spite of my over-developed sense of "social appropriateness" which kept telling me to "ssshhh."

Probably two months or so after our initial meeting, Tim mentioned that he would enjoy spending some time with me outside of church. He also informed me that he had chosen me as "his" pastor. (This particular church had six full-time members of the pastoral team—so I supposed Tim figured he could pick any of them to be "his" pastor. That was me.) We determined that we would have lunch together that next week. We agreed that I would come by his work to pick him up.

Two days later, I showed up at the local Wal-Mart to find Tim. Before we left his store, however, he wanted to introduce me to several of his associates. I agreed, and off we went on a whirlwind tour of each department. It was like I was a local celebrity or something. He was so proud to walk around introducing "his" pastor to all the people he knew (and even some he didn't know)! As we walked, Tim told me all about being an employee at Wal-Mart. He genuinely loved working there and felt that he was treated well by the management. He told me about the regular meetings he attended and the various purchases he had made since beginning to work there. He was especially proud of a computer he had bought for his son. Tim explained how it would help him in school. I could tell Tim was a good dad who cared deeply about his children.

We finished up our tour, and drove to a local pizza place that had an "all you can eat" lunch special. Tim seemed to me to be the type that might have a big appetite, and I wanted to make sure he got enough food.

We each filled our plates with pizza and salad and sat down together. I asked Tim to pray with me and he humbly bowed his head. After I said "Amen," Tim immediately wanted to know more about praying. Our conversation began with how I prayed and what prayer was. I again explained to Tim that the words we say to God are just like any other conversation we might have with a friend. They do not need to be scripted or perfect, just honest. From there, our conversation meandered to various topics: the church, being a pastor, my education, etc. Then he plainly asked how much the church paid me to pray on Sundays. I smiled, and explained that my job was quite a bit more extensive than praying on Sunday during the service, and I answered his question directly. I figured if Tim asked a straight question, I ought to honor that with a straight answer. Typically people do not ask such direct questions—it's not considered polite—but Tim was not like most people.

He did not dress like most people, talk like most people, nor did he associate with only the "right" people, and frankly, it was quite refreshing for me to have a friend like Tim. Tim thought out loud that maybe he should look into becoming a pastor, since my salary was more than he made at Wal-Mart.

Since I worked in a church and mostly associated with "church" people, the folks that I was around were quite proper, and did the socially acceptable and appropriate thing. Being around Tim, however, it became quite clear that he had not been instructed about what is socially acceptable and appropriate. This did not make Tim unacceptable—rather, it made him real, unvarnished, and honest. He had a certain edge to him. At times a cuss word might slip from his lips. In most cases, it was not an attempt to be profane, but rather to honestly express his emotion. It is not that churched people are not honest, but sometimes in the name of being kind or loving, we speak less than the whole truth. This way of living simply did not occur to Tim. He was direct and straight. He said what he felt. He expressed his doubts, questions, and fears sincerely and openly—albeit sometimes a bit coarsely.

As our friendship grew, so did the frequency of our visits and interaction. One day, Tim invited me to come by his house. When I arrived and knocked on the door, the way Tim welcomed me in reminded me of several months prior when we walked through Wal-Mart for the first time together. Tim was so excited that I had come to his house, and it showed. He had a way of making a person know they were appreciated and loved, just for being his friend. His girlfriend Kara was there, and it was very obvious that she was expecting. In fact, she was due about the same time my wife was going to deliver. Their house was humble, but homey. In typical form, Tim gave me a tour and while I listened to him.

I noticed a lot of stuff all around, but it wasn't particularly dirty. There were pictures, too. One was of Tim on a beautiful Harley Davidson motorcycle and one was of an outlaw-looking character that Tim told me was the president of the Southern California Chapter of the Hells Angels. He talked about their friendship and the stuff they used to do together. We came to Tim and Kara's bedroom. Tim seemed a bit embarrassed that he and Kara shared this room and house together, since they were not married. He talked briefly about marrying her and asked me if I could perform the wedding. I told him I could and that I would be honored to, should they decide they wanted to make that important step.

It was obvious that whatever Tim wanted to show me was going to happen quite soon. He reached into a closet and pulled out a rather intimidating looking weapon. Tim informed me it was an AK-47. He said it was one of many of his guns, but his most prized possession. I didn't know what to say. I didn't know if this was an illegal weapon or what. I was basically speechless. I had thought he wanted to show me a car he was working on at his house or some other sort of project. Instead, he showed me this, and I was uncharacteristically without words. I managed to spit out something sort of lame like, "Tell me about this gun, Tim," and so he did.

When he finished telling me all about it, I had regained my composure enough to ask him the purpose for owning a gun like this. He said it was for protection. I wondered what he might need protecting from, but as I reflected on his relationship with the Hells Angels Motorcycle Club, I began to get a picture.

I thanked Tim for his hospitality and for inviting me to his home. I said my goodbyes to his son, and Kara and Tim walked me to my car. He told me how much he appreciated me coming by, and that I was his friend. He sort of got choked up, then said goodbye. As he turned away from me to walk back to his house, I noticed he wiped his eyes.

In the coming weeks, it was more of the same with Tim. We would talk occasionally during the week, he might stop by my office, and then on Sunday Tim and Kara would sit with us at church. Often Tim would put large bills into the offering plate as it passed by him. I could not help but notice, and wonder how he was getting money like that.

My wife, Sandy, was in her final weeks before our first child was to be born. We were busily making the final arrangements for the arrival. One night the phone rang, and it was Tim; Kara had gone into labor that morning and delivered a baby boy—Sloan—and he wondered if I would come to visit them. Sandy and I quickly jumped into the car to visit our friends.

I had never seen Tim as proud or as loving as I did that evening. He was so proud of his new son Sloan, and so loving toward his girlfriend Kara, who had given him his second child. Sandy and I both held Sloan and oooed and aaahed over their beautiful child. I could not help but wonder if Sloan and our soon-to-be-born child would be friends. We stayed for several minutes, prayed for the new family, and then gave hugs all around before leaving.

Several weeks after our son Spencer was born, we invited Kara and Tim to our house to spend some time together. Tim could not make it, but Kara, Sloan, and Tim's son Richard ended up coming. Spencer and Sloan were just babies but they sort of "played" together. As we visited, Kara explained that Tim had quit working at Wal-Mart several weeks before. I immediately inquired how they were paying the hospital bills, not to mention buying groceries. She said, rather cryptically, that Tim had some other work he was doing, but would not elaborate. Sensing her hesitation, I left it at that. It was not a particularly long visit, but cordial. Kara collected her son and Richard and headed out to their car.

Several days after that visit, Tim called me at home. He was very upset and talking rapidly. He kept saying how he had "really screwed up." He said he was in jail. He had been caught with a bunch of drugs and it did not look good for him. I was not completely surprised by the news. In some ways, it made sense—the lack of a job but money still coming in, the large bills he had been putting into the offering at church . . . I was very concerned for what this meant for Tim and his family. I asked him about the drugs and his involvement with them. He was incredibly remorseful. He explained that he was offered a lot of money to simply "drop" them off at a pre-determined place occasionally; although he knew it was wrong, the allure of a bunch of cash was too much for him to resist. He apologized to me, and through tears vowed to never do anything like this again. I told him that was a good start, and that he needed to talk to God about the things he had done. Tim agreed, and asked me if I was still going to be his friend. I knew this was a significant point in our relationship. I assured him that regardless of what came from all of this, I would certainly remain his friend and see him through this situation. What I did not know when I made that promise was the extent and duration of the legal issues in which Tim was now involved. Tim explained that he was being held at the county jail and he pleaded with me to visit him. I told him I would come the next day and we could talk. That helped him calm a bit. I prayed with him on the phone and told him I would see him the next day.

When I got in to see Tim early the next afternoon, he was delighted to see me, and tears immediately welled up in his eyes. Then he told me the whole story. We each sat down on opposite sides of a booth, with thick glass separating us. What had happened, Tim explained, is that he had been offered a deal a few months before to make a "drop" for a friend of his—for $1,000. All he had to do was to take a package from a point A to point B. His friend did not tell him what was in the package, just that it was very valuable and worth a lot of money for him. Tim had a very clear idea what the package would contain, but managed to rationalize that he would only do it once and the money would help him provide a nice Christmas for his family. In fact, he told me he gave a significant part of the money to the church after buying gifts for Kara and Richard! He asked me if that was wrong, and I assured him that God can redeem anything, even drug money. Anyway, he went on to tell me that after Christmas he lost his job at Wal-Mart, so the temptation to make some quick cash got the best of him.

The pressure of the hospital bills just added to the ease of rationalizing just "one more drop." The funny thing, Tim said, was that when he was stopped by the police, it had nothing to do with the drugs he had put into Sloan's diaper bag. He had a taillight out, and when the police stopped him, the bag was accidentally kicked over and the package fell out. When Tim saw that, he started acting sort of panicked, and the police quickly picked up on that. In no time, they asked him to step out of the car. They searched it, and quickly discovered a large quantity of Methamphetamine.

From that stop, he was taken directly to jail, and that was when he called me. I asked Tim if he had a lawyer, and what the next steps were. He said he did not know precisely yet, but that he would likely have a trial in a few weeks. He said a public defender would represent him, since he really did not have any money to hire a lawyer. He had been living "large," but now all the money needed to be saved for Kara and the two children. He was most likely going to prison, and wanted to provide what little he could for them.

This was all pretty overwhelming to me. I had been a pastor for about eight years at the time; I had visited people in jail, been inside prisons, but all this was just surreal. This family that I knew, and had grown to love, was being split apart through some very foolish behavior on Tim's part—now they would all pay for it. It seemed so unfair that just as his son Richard was getting along so well at church and people were really investing in this family, he had to go and do something so stupid. I was both angry and deeply sorry for him. I knew he really wanted to be a good father and husband, but got caught up in the idea of making fast money. I struggled to know exactly how to act toward him. On the one hand, I wanted to punch him. On the other, I wanted to hug him—particularly when the tears came—and tell him it was all going to be alright. I had a hard time imagining Jesus punching anyone, so I decided I might be better off showing Tim love. Frankly, he was beating himself up pretty good; he probably needed me to offer him some love, so that's what I decided to do from that day forward.

At the end of our visit that day, I told him that I loved him, and again reassured him that I would walk through this with him, regardless of how long it took. I visited Tim and Kara as often as I could in the coming weeks. It was a commitment to be his friend through this trial. I tried my best to keep in contact with Kara too, but her mom and dad lived in town, so they made sure she was doing alright. I felt that I could not give up on Tim and his family, although there were days when I considered it. (I am not proud to admit that, but it was a truthful part of this journey and needs to be said.)

Tim made it very clear to me that he wanted me to be at each part of the trial. I told him I would do what I was able, and he was always very understanding and respectful. When those events did actually come around, I was at each one.

Tim was found guilty of trafficking drugs; because our state had been engaged in a battle against Meth for many years, there were mandatory sentencing statutes. Due to the amount of Meth that Tim was carrying, he was going to jail for at least five years, and there was simply no way around that. At the sentencing, Tim told his lawyer how his pastor was in the courtroom and, in desperation, he called me up to the witness stand as a character witness for Tim. After being sworn in, I was asked a few questions about Tim, and even allowed to address the court. I simply asked for him to be allowed to work to support his family while he was in jail. That simply was not going to happen, but I could not help but make that request on his behalf. I knew that was his single most difficult issue in all this—he did not want Kara and the kids to pay the price for his sins. Unfortunately, that is not the way the law works. Tim was sentenced to serve 5 - 15 years (to be reviewed after 5), and he would begin that sentence in five days.

Tim invited me to his house for his "going to jail party" a couple of days later. When I showed, the party was in full swing. Tim was in the back barbequing, and there was a sort of self-service bar available with soda and beer. The house was not packed, but there were several people there that I did not know. When I entered his house, true to form, Tim proudly introduced me to each of his friends. The looks on some of their faces when Tim told them I was his pastor were priceless! It was as if I was an alien with some sort of primordial ooze on my hand as they shook it. All of a sudden, I went from being uncomfortable in the crowd to the crowd being uncomfortable around me. It was a very strange, and yet very good place for me to be—in the middle of real people's lives, as Jesus always was.

I learned later that the people who gathered that night to eat and drink with Tim, Kara, and the kids were a lot of Tim's associates from the Meth trade. I also later learned that not one of them visited him, or really even kept in touch with him within 12 months of his incarceration.

After the party, things got pretty difficult for both Tim and Kara. Tim, of course, went to jail. Over the course of the next four and a half years, Tim was moved seven different times to various facilities. The distances from our community ranged from about fifteen minutes to over four hours away! Tim relied pretty heavily on Kara for money during this time, and that led to a significant strain on their relationship. (In prison there are several things that can be purchased at the "store"—from snacks to shaving cream and envelopes to socks—they could be purchased once each week. I got quite an education about the criminal justice system as I walked with Tim through this process.) I kept our pastoral team apprised of Tim's situation and his sincere need for a bit of money for envelopes, paper, and stamps—since letters were his primary connection with the outside world. Our church decided to sponsor Tim at the rate of $25 per month to help cover some of these expenses. It wasn't much, but it made all the difference to Tim. He often thanked me for it through tears.

We exchanged letters frequently during his first couple of years, and I visited him as often as I could, which wasn't very much, actually. I often had guilt about it too—which Tim always dismissed quickly when I expressed it. He would say, "I know you have a wife and kids, Mike. Don't worry about it."

Life was not easy for Tim, but things got even tougher for Kara. First, there was the need for Kara to find work and child care for an infant. She had not done much work outside of the fast-food industry, so that is where she ended up again. Then there were the long drives to see Tim on the weekends with two children. Next, there was the custody trial for Richard, since Kara was not his biological mother. Although Richard's mom was employed in a less than desirable industry (she worked as a dancer in Las Vegas), the decision went in her favor. So she flew in from Las Vegas to pick him up. I was there with Kara when Child Services came and took him away. It was awful. Everyone was crying and eventually screaming. I would be happy to never witness that again. With all this stress in Kara's life, it is no wonder their relationship did not make it through Tim's first year in prison. Then Tim was alone, or at least he felt that way. In some ways, that might have been the very best thing for him. He began regularly reading his Bible. At first, a few verses each night; in time, several chapters each day. Tim knew that God was near him—I was always telling him things like that. Now he finally decided to start paying attention. It wasn't long until Tim started telling me about the things he was reading; he was even planning how he was going to serve God when he got out of prison. I was delighted see this experience of grace that Tim was discovering.

One of Tim's moves brought him very close to our town, to a facility with a lot of privileges and freedom. Tim had been a model prisoner and was able, after only 2 years, to come to the "Farm," which is a work-release facility. I was able to have barbeques with him and even order pizza while we visited. Always in our visits, Tim was talking about reading his Bible and how he wanted to serve God when he got out. Now, I am not sure Tim ever said the actual words "serve God," but that was exactly what he talked about. He wanted to work with me, to talk to young people about drugs and the dangers of getting involved with them. Tim wanted to share not only his story, but his life with anyone who would listen. He experienced great pain, being isolated from the first five years of Sloan's life, and from other family and friends. He wanted to tell others about that pain, to help them avoid similar mistakes.

Tim also often recounted in our visits how he had no one left in his life. None of his friends who were always around him when he was "dealing" were around now. They all left when the drugs dried up. He had no one—no one, that is, except the church that supported him and two friends from that church who visited him—Slim Henry and myself. Tim often spoke about the support he received from us as if it was something truly special. He knew he could count on us, and I like to believe he sensed God's presence when we were with him.

This was the way life was for Tim for four long years. He was in the system, and didn't have much say about what happened to him from day to day. He did his best to keep himself out of trouble and simply "do his time."

And then, in the fifth year of his sentence, several things came together. First, a letter from an old female friend came in the mail for Tim. He had no idea how she found him, but there had been "sparks" in the past, and in no time the two of them, through letters and visits, were dating. Then, Tim worked successfully to get Richard back to our town to stay with his sister. He would have his son waiting for him when he got out! And lastly, since he was in his final year of incarceration, he was able to get a job. He got placed with a modular home building company and found a position that he loved. It seemed that all that was taken away when he went to jail was now coming back as he was preparing to leave prison. It was just like God, I told him, to redeem what seemed unredeemable and to bring beauty from the ashes that we sometimes experience. Unfortunately, Kara did not want to have any contact with Tim. She had moved on in her life and was unwilling to allow Sloan any sort of relationship with him. That weighed heavily on Tim's heart, but that story is not finished yet.

Tim recently called, and through tears told me the exact date he would be released. He informed me that I ought to write it on my calendar since I would be picking him up that day! I was delighted to be asked/told that I was his ride home.

Of course, the story is not over for Tim. I trust that he will make good on the promise to stay clean and make an honest living, once released. I truly believe he will. But, in any case, I am his friend and his brother in Christ and will stand by him—as I believe Jesus would.

Tim is a believer and follower of Jesus Christ now. I am not sure when he actually made that commitment. The fact that he considers how Jesus would want him to respond to the people and situations he encounters is the evidence of his growing relationship. Jesus tells us in John 14:23, "If anyone loves me, he will obey my teaching. My Father will love him, and we will come to him and make our home with him." Tim is proving his love for Jesus daily as he obeys Christ's teaching.

We have been exploring in this book what it means to be Kingdom people, and what it means to share our faith with our friends. Some call that evangelism. This book emphasizes an approach to evangelism that is based on friendship and relationship. There are many ways that we can do evangelism, but I want to offer you the story of Tim as one (perhaps new) way to think about it and approach it. Friendship evangelism is very much about who we are and the kind of friend we are. It is a lifestyle of offering ourselves to others more than it is about having a script to share. It is about seeing the image of God in people, and loving them into the Kingdom. It may take time and effort. It certainly means allowing the Spirit of God to lead us. But in many ways it means simply being a friend to someone on their journey, and being there for them when they need you.

I do not believe Tim would have responded well to a confrontational approach to sharing faith, although that has worked for many in the past. I don't know how Tim would have responded if someone told him that he needed to accept Jesus or he was going to hell. In many ways, Tim knew what hell was like through the life he had lived. I think that given time and love, he has learned well that eternal life, the abundant life, does not begin when you die, but when you follow Jesus. Tim learned that while locked in prison, and for the first time he was truly free.

CHAPTER 7
FINAL THOUGHTS

ON FRIENDSHIP EVANGELISM

If evangelism is to be reclaimed as a way of being, then we must change the way we think about it. We must become intentional in how we choose to be in the world. Instead of trying to invent new ways to get non-church people to come to church and to adopt church culture, we must meet people out in their culture. If the purpose of the church is to be a catalyst for Kingdom, then we should be inviting people to join us in relationship first, because that is what the Kingdom is built upon. We are seeking to be the church by being a friend.[19]

The church receives its breath for life from prayer, passion, and purpose—purpose founded in the directive of the Beatitudes for inheriting the Kingdom. Here brokenness is good. Weakness is strength. Preachers are poets and propagandists of grace—spilling the beans on the easy yoke of Christ, and setting disciples of Christ free from legalism.

BECOMING

Becoming His dream for the church must be done in process—serving our community with no expectations of return. We teach this by being it. It is a sort of "on the way" training.

Being the church requires more than coming to a building. It means more service to others than to ourselves. It's a day-to-day experience of desperation in the spirit of Christ that saturates every corner of our lives with the grace of Jesus—so thick that we live and move and have our being in the love of God, so saturated that we operate from the foundational idea that we are loved.

MISSIONAL

We can no longer wait and hope in a central location, asking others to come and join us, but must use that central location as a launching pad for grace lavished on our community. We must be a people of creative energies. As a missional people we are to become lost in the love of Christ, give without caution, serve as the only way of life, and be emptied of all but humility in order to lavish love on the world through actions of insane sacrifice. We are a church of people that move in Christ with a focus of meeting the brokenness of the world in the midst of its mess, and not create its own mess in the midst of the world. Jesus is already present and active, healing the world in many ways. Let's find where He is moving and ask how we can come alongside of what Jesus is already accomplishing for the Kingdom. Let's renew an initiative of cooperating with Jesus' kingdom in our culture.

As the world around us changes rapidly, Jesus must be our center. If He is not, our center will move with the next tech upgrade or cultural trend. We must be present, and navigate these currents to meet Jesus in the midst of the "unknown gods" of our culture, among its efforts to find purpose and meaning. We must always live Jesus-focused, self-giving, and other-serving.

I've heard people say, when referring to end times, they have read the back of the book and we win. I understand the faith and hope of Christ's final victory, but the Kingdom life is very much about life now, not just living for the future. Jesus is seeking, in His grace, to redeem all of humanity. Not just the "winners," and not just the church. He wants to redeem all of creation! Sometimes we get fixated on how things are going to end, and are concerned about heaven or hell or the next life, and neglect the present. Jesus talked about these things, but He was also very concerned with the Kingdom come—now. His Father's kingdom is open and available to all who have eyes to see and ears to hear. Christ calls us to live this Kingdom come . . . now. Here is a summary of the ideas in this book from the heart of a student from our local youth group:

Throughout my life, I have dealt with a lot of hardships, but in every one God was there to keep me on my feet. My journey with Christ is one of doubt and realization. Throughout my teen years, I have strayed away from the path that he has laid before me, but at the same time I have begun to realize many things about God and the things he has done for me. I have found a Savior that died not only for me, or other churchgoers, but the murderers, rapists, Muslims, Jews, terrorists and politicians. We're all people who are called by one name, Beloved.

—Anonymous 16 year-old

In all our relationships, we can share that love, being a reminder—a catalyst—a friend who reminds others of the love of Jesus, and the Kingdom life that He offers them, if they are willing to receive it.

BEING REAL

In the end, *being real* means that if a person is a follower of Jesus, then in every single decision that person makes, it is their genuine aim to follow the will of Christ. If we claim to be a follower of Him, then all that we do should follow His will, first and foremost. The way we live is worthy of someone who is made in the image of God. To be Christian means all we do is marked by our identity as a child of God and follower of Jesus Christ.

To be Christian ought to mean that we cultivate relationships on purpose, as Jesus did. We love all people, since we are all children of the King. The places we visit, we seek to be a missionary there. Even then, our goal is not to "win people to Jesus." Our goal is to love God and love those around us. As a part of that, we are happy to tell our friends (and all with whom we have a relationship) what God has done for us.

How do we share our faith? Be a friend. Care for them, spend time with them, and let the Kingdom in you rub off on them. Don't worry about what you will say to them, because as you follow Jesus closely, His Spirit will lead you and guide you. Share your faith as you have opportunity, but be real—you don't have to force it upon them. Pray and trust and let God work.

OUR RELATIONSHIP TO THE WORLD

God told Abram in Genesis 12 that He was going to bless him, so that Abram would be a blessing to the world. I am concerned that we have forgotten our connection to Abram and this promise. The church is not for us. At least, it is not exclusively for those of us who are followers of Jesus. It is for the benefit of those people that are loved by God, but are still outside church walls. The church is also for those people who are still unaware of God's unimaginable love for them.

Our part is to allow God to direct our steps in a way that others may know the reality of God's love. Our whole lives, careers, marriages, schedules, plans, dreams, relationships, vacations, and purchases are to be infused with this reality.

So in the end, *being real* means being real with Jesus Christ—which utterly shapes every area of our lives. And it really goes deeper than that. Paul the Apostle has said it best in Colossians 3:1-3, "Therefore if you have been raised up with Christ, keep seeking the things above, where Christ is seated at the right hand of God. Set your mind on the things above, not on the things that are on earth. *For you have died and your life is hidden with Christ in God.*" [emphasis added]. As Christ-followers, our lives have ended; now they are hidden in Christ. It is time that we begin letting the life of Christ live through us, in all its intended impact. That impact will influence the way we treat others and everything else we do every day. That kind of life is one where faith is shared easily and regularly—because it flows out of the Spirit of Christ in us. We love God and love our neighbors and our lives show it. Nothing could be more real.

NOTES

1. A paraphrase of a newspaper article by Terrance Petty in a Feb 2007 issue of the *Idaho Press Tribune.*

2. <http://bible.crosswalk.com/Lexicons/Greek/grk.cgi?number=2099&version=nas>, accessed March 2, 2007

3. <http://bible.crosswalk.com/Lexicons/Greek/grk.cgi?number=2098&version=nas>, accessed March 2, 2007

4. *Rev!* Sept/Oct (2006): 19 Group Publishing

5. Ibid.

6. Genesis 2:27

7. Matthew 5:13-16

8. To say that humans are made in the image of God is to recognize the special qualities of human nature, which allow God to be made manifest in humans. <http://www.meta-library.net/theogloss/imago-body.html>, accessed March 2, 2007.

9. <www.ymsp.org>

10. <http://jewsforjesus.org/judaica/Passover>, accessed March 2, 2007.

11. Matthew 22:37-40

12. Matthew 5:43-48

13. 2 Corinthians 1:3-4

14. John Drane's book, *"Do Christians Know How to Be Spiritual?"* (published by Darton, Longman and Todd: London, England 2005) is an excellent resource and tool in understanding this phenomena.

15. <http://www.lucidcafe.com/library/96mar/michelangelo.htOml> accessed March 12, 2007

16. Bonhoeffer, Dietrich. *Life Together,* Harper Collins 1954 p. 35

17. Not his real name

18. Mark 2:27-28

19. This thought was inspired the reading of an article by Bill Easum in the Jan/Feb 2007 issue of *Rev!* magazine and another article by Thomas G. Bandy in the Sept/Oct 2007 issue of *NETResults* magazine.